DIG IT!

A DIRECTORY OF FEE-BASIS ROCK COLLECTING SITES OPEN TO AMATEURS

BY

CAROL E. KINDLER
P.O. Box 12328
PHILADELPHIA, PA 19119

Sixth Edition

ISBN 0-943502-03-9

Dig It !

**A DIRECTORY OF
FEE-BASIS
ROCK COLLECTING SITES
OPEN TO AMATEURS**

by CAROL E. KINDLER

TABLE OF CONTENTS

INTRODUCTION

My husband, Leonard, and I have been rockhounding for some years, and have found that a digging site with an owner to call for directions saves time, trouble, and gas--not to mention tempers. If you plan to write for information, I recommend that you write well in advance of your trip, to give the owner time to answer. Also, be sure to include a stamped return envelope when writing for information. Many places close unexpectedly due to illness or death in the family; some are sold, and the new owners may not permit digging.

This edition incorporates several new features and organizational changes. For the first time, Canadian digging sites are included. Also, for the first time there is a section on related literature and maps covering a single collecting area (mainly individual states). There is information available for areas like Nebraska that have no fee-basis sites, and do not appear in the main listing. City and state addresses to write to for additional information on rockhunting and/or tourism have been grouped together in another new section. I also suggest you write to the Chamber of Commerce of a town, or to an area rock club, if you need more help. Unfortunately, two states reported that their rockhunting booklets (Dig Me, from Maine, and South Carolina Minerals and Gems) were out of print.

I have listed the main minerals found at each location in a separate column, so you can look for a particular mineral or get an idea of what is available in an area. I am again including a separate list of places that I know to be closed. Some of them were in previous editions of this book; others were well-known free sites. Please remember that the sites listed in this book are Private Property. Publication of their addresses DOES NOT entitle you to collect at these sites. In each case, permission must be obtained from the owner and the required fees paid before collecting. Treat sites with the proper respect. Don't leave garbage lying about on someone else's property, and do not damage any structure. Observe common-sense safety precautions; careless digging can result in injuries to yourself and others.

I would like to thank all the people who sent information for this book. Many wrote long letters and included maps and pictures. Rockhounds and mine owners seem to be the friendliest people in the world. Special thanks are due to my husband, who made many valuable suggestions, gave me encouragement, did the final editing, typed the copy for the printer, and handled all the business arrangements. Thanks, too, to John Volk, for his illustration for the front cover.

SPECIAL NOTE

**Information for sites marked with a double asterisk is incomplete because the owners did not respond to mail inquiries. These sites are, however, believed to be open. If you are in the area on a trip, by all means check them out. Any new information you can send me about these sites will be very much appreciated, and will be used to improve future editions of this book.

DIGGING SITES ARE ARRANGED BY STATES, AND THEN BY TOWNS
WHERE THE MINES ARE LOCATED (UNDERLINED), IN ALPHABETICAL
ORDER. SEE INTRODUCTION FOR THE MEANING OF THE ** SYMBOL.

DIGGING SITE	MINERALS

ALASKA

Stewart's Jewel Jade Claims, located
at Dahl Creek. Stewart's Photo
Shop, 531 4th Ave., Anchorage, AK
99501. Phone (907) 272-8581. Open
June & July. Camping and cabins
avail.; make reserv. 3 months in
advance. No fee for digging.
    Jade, gold, serpentine, quartz, asbestos, rhodonite, chrysoprase

**Atlanta House, Glenn Highway, Mile 166.
M. C. White, SS Rt C-280, Palmer,
AK 99645.
    Fossils

**Garnet Ledge, Wrangell. Write to
Southeast Alaska Council, Boy
Scouts of America, Inc., P.O. Box
510, Juneau, AK 99802 for information and authorization forms.
Groups only. Fee: $3.50. Phone
(907) 586-1785.
    Garnets

ARIZONA

Patton & Sons, P.O. Box 908, Holbrook,
AZ 86025. Phone (602) 524-3470.
Open all year, 7 days a week, 6 AM-
8 PM. Free camping for self-contained. Fees: $15/person for up
to 30 lbs. 50¢/lb. over 30 lbs.
    Petrified wood

CLOSED Oatman Fire Agate, Box 900, "O" Star
Rt., Kingman, AZ 86401. Mrs. Anna
Cuesta. Open all year. Fee: $2.00
each. Camping $1.00.
    Fire agate, desert roses

Fire Agate Claims. Mr. James P. Erick-
son, P.O. Box 37, Oatman, AZ 86433.
Phone (602) 768-4392. Fee: $2.00/
person/day. Camping: contact Alma
Snyder, (602) 768-4392.
    Fire agate

Richey's Rocks, 2nd W. 6th No., St.
John's, AZ 85936. Phone 337-4596.
Minimum 25 lbs. @ 40¢/lb.
    Flower agate, snowflake agate, amethyst, "man- ganese crystals"

Apache Tear Caves, Box 7, Superior,
AZ 85273. Phone 689-5101 or 689-
5541. Fee: $1.00/gallon bucket.
    Apache tears (translucent ob- sidian)

ARKANSAS

Clark Runyan, Shady Heights Road, Rt. 6, Box 194, <u>Hot Springs</u>, AR 71901. Phone (501) 262-2058. Fee: $2.00.
   Black quartz, "Coontail" quartz, titanium with brookite Garnet

**<u>Magnet Cove</u> (on U.S. 270 east of Hot Springs). State-operated 30-acre garnet field.

Crystal City, Inc., S.R. 1, Box 136A, <u>Mt. Ida</u>, AR 71957. Mr. David Lebow. Phone (501) 867-3266. Open all year. Fee: $5.00/day. Primitive camping (no fee).
   Quartz crystals

Ocus Stanly, P.O. Box 163, <u>Mt. Ida</u>, AR 71957. Phone (501) 867-5266. Fee: "What it is worth to you."(Suggested minimum: $1.50) Open all year.
   Quartz crystals

**Starfire Mine, Mr. Charlie Burch, <u>Mt. Ida</u>, AR 71957.
   Quartz crystals

Crater of Diamonds State Park, Rt. 1, Box 364, <u>Murfreesboro</u>, AR 71958. Phone (501) 285-3113. Fee: $2.00.
   Diamond, opal, agate, quartz, amethyst, calcite

**Rush Zinc Mine, Mr. Fred Dirst, Guide, <u>Yellville</u>, AR 72687.
   Smithsonite

CALIFORNIA

Earth Arts, 5262 Fern Flat Road, <u>Aptos</u>, CA 95003. Write for latest information.
   Field trips

**A. Willson, Box 281, <u>Baker</u>, CA 92309. "Sheep-Creek Camp." No fees. Near several good sites.
   Pearlescent, translucent marble; petrified palm wood; owl-hole agate

Ron Everett, Ron's Rocks, 33 Willden Dr., Camarillo, CA 93010. Phone (805) 482-4330. Mine is in <u>Baker</u>, CA. Open all year. Make advance arrangements. Fee: 50¢/lb.; 75¢ pre-dug. Free camping with $5.00 rock purchase.
   Cave onyx, stalactites, "Legendary Kokoweef Caverns"

Stewart Lithia Mine, J. Springer, Box 23, <u>Bonsall</u>, CA 92003. Phone (714) 722-2783. Open Sat. or Sun. Bring shovels & screens. Write for map and brochure. Advance reservations needed. Fees: $7.50 per adult; $2.50/child under 13 yrs. old for up to 10 lbs. Camping $2.50/night.
   Tourmaline, quartz, mica, albite, amblygonite, garnet, lepidolite, others

Gloria Mine, near Boron, CA. Write Maja Mines, 9714 Cozycroft Ave., Chatsworth, CA 91311. Phone (213) 998-6105. Open all year, by reservation, to clubs and organizations. Fees: $10 for each 50 lbs. or 50¢/lb. for smaller quantities. Free camping.
Picture agate & jasper (once called the "Calico Jasper Picture Rock Mine")

**U.S. Borax Mine, Borax Rd., Boron, CA. Collecting on dumps on weekends when mine is not operating. Check at main gate for permission, map, release forms, and schedule.
Ulexite, calcite, colemanite, realgar, borax, kernite

Red Jasper Mine. Rachel Herzog, Star Rt. 3, Box 47, Coalinga, CA 93210. Phone (209) 935-0628. Fee: 25¢/lb. Minimum of 10 per group. Open 9-5, closed August for deer season. Fee for camping $1/day; $2.00 for vehicles with trailer. Call first.
Jasper--many colors

**Mariposite Quarry (Mariposa). Mr. Dolph Jacobs, Coulterville, CA 95311. Mine is on State Hwy. 49. Fee: 5¢/lb. Phone (209) 532-4543. Call first to have gate opened.
Mariposite

**Dryden Ranch, Eel River Rd., Covelo, CA 95428.
Jade

Keekay No. 1 Mine. Ms. Kathryn Burrow, P.O. Box 968, Eldridge, CA 95431. Phone (707) 546-6491. Open all yr. No fee, but ask permission to dig.
Jasp-agate, petrified palm wood, opal

Stifle Claim, Georgetown. Send SASE to Alonzo Gust, Box 402, Diamond Springs, CA 95619 for map and permit. Phone (916) 622-3446 before 8 AM or after 10 PM. Fee: $2/person/day. Free camping; no hookups; bring water.
Epidote, antigorite, serpentine, diopside, garnet, jade, quartz

Rainbow Mine, Inyo County, CA. Write for appt. to Mr. Rusty Springer, 6524 Bourbon Way, Las Vegas, NV 89107. Phone (702) 878-2392. Open to clubs Sept. to June. Fee: 50¢/lb.
Inyo rainbow onyx

**Karl Kubik, Iowa Hill, CA (near Colfax). Fee: $3.00 for 20 lbs. + 25¢ for each additional pound.
Tremolite ("California tigereye")

**Spider Mine, Novato, CA 94947. New owner: Mr. Walter Koniuk, 1263 42nd Ave., San Francisco, CA 94122.
Rhodonite, rhodochrosite

Feather River Pastimes. Mr. Frank C. Wagoner, Box 899, <u>Oroville</u>, CA 95965. Phone (916) 533-0988. Rocks free. Camping $2.00; cabins $7.50/day for 2 people. Gold panning $1.00/car. Reservations required for cabins. — Gold, jade

Jade International, Mrs. Leza Junnila, Clear Creek Road, <u>Paicines</u>, CA 95043. Open all year. Free camping. Write to be sure someone is there. Bring water. Guided trips, $10/person; unguided $3/person. Under 12 yrs. old free. — Jadeite, serpentine, plasma agate, cinnabar

Opal Hill Mine, Helen Madden, Box 232, <u>Palo Verde</u>, CA 92266. Phone (714) 922-6256. $10/day, $40/week, $80/month. Wife & kids under 16 free. Open Oct. 15 to May 1. Camping available. — Fire agate

**Fossil Art Creations, Russell F. Shoemaker, Jr., P.O. Box 4263, <u>Pasadena</u>, CA 91101. — Fossils

Stifle Memorial Claims. El Dorado County Mineral & Gem Society, P.O. Box 950, <u>Placerville</u>, CA 95667. Mr. Arthur Martin, phone (916) 622-1762. Fee: $2.00 for 20 lbs.; 25¢/lb. over that. Dry camping incl. in fee. — Asbestos, chalcedony, idocrase, jade, serpentine, quartz crystals, brown garnet, tremolite

**South Indian Jade Claims, Eva Rosin, 4270 Silver Crest Ave., <u>Sacramento</u>, CA 95821. Phone (916) 482-0168. — Garnet, idocrase, jade, serpentine, marble, actinolite

**Chan Jade Mine. Happy Camp, Valley of the Moon Gem Club, Box 583, <u>Sonoma</u>, CA. Fee: $2.00. — Idocrase, nephrite

Antelope Canyon Ranch, Mr. & Mrs. Wyman, Box 253, <u>Tehachapi</u>, CA 93561. Phone (805) 822-3125. May 31 to Sept. 30, weekends only, but will open for large groups other days. Fee: $1.00. Camping with showers. — Marble, limestone, garnets

**Patricks Point State Park, <u>Trinidad</u>, CA. Fee: $2/day/car. Limit of 50 lbs. of rock per day per person. Camping, $4.00/night. — Agate, jasper, petrified wood, jade

Delia & Fletscher Tweed, Box 395, <u>Trona</u>, CA 93562. Open Sept. 1 to May 31. Fee: 25¢/lb. Camping, 50¢/night. — Calcite onyx

Mack Mine. Mrs. L. Hall, Star Route,   Tourmaline
Box 190, Valley Center, CA 92082.
Phone (714) 749-0635. Closed July &
August. Fee: $2/person. Camping $5
each. No children or pets unless
kept in trailer. Make reservations
three weeks in advance.

Double Springs Gem Rocks. Ed & Thelma   Moss agate, den-
Hale, Box 207, Valley Springs, CA   dritic opal, my-
95252. Phone (209) 772-2127. Open   rickite, many
all year. Write or call ahead. Fee: colors of den-
$4/person/day up to 30 lbs. 30¢/lb.   dritic agate
over that. Camping $2/night; $5/
night with electric hookup.

Valley Springs Ranch. John & Betty   Serpentine, moss
Snyder, Box 177, Valley Springs, CA agate, opal, jas-
95252. Phone (209) 772-1265. Call   per, Calif. jade
for information. Closed except for
once-a-year Pow-Wow, with digging.

COLORADO

**Rocky Mountain Natural Science, Box   Field trips
3302, Boulder, CO 80307.

Turquoise Queen Mine, Mr. Ben R.   Turquoise
O'Haver, Box 25, Cripple Creek, CO
80813. Phone (303) 689-2253. Open
May 30 to Oct. 15, 10 AM-3 PM. Fee:
$15/day; $10/half day. Discounts
for groups of 10 or more.

**Indian Crafts & Construction Co.,   Fossils
Florissant, CO 80816.

Mile Hi Minerals, 195 Mesa Verde,   Amazonstone,
Golden, CO 80401. Phone (303) 279- smoky quartz,
7302. Open May 25 to Sept. 5;   green fluorite,
closed Mondays. Fees: Main pit,   albite, topaz,
$17.50/day; $10.00/half day.   goethite
Screening area, $1.50/hr. Field
trips by advance reservation.

Turquoise Chief Mine. Mr. Norman Reed, Turquoise
Sugar Loafin' Campground, MMSR 310,
Leadville, CO 80461. May 30 thru
Sept. Phone (303) 486-1031; winter
486-1613. Fees: $10 for 2 1/2 hrs.
$15 for 5 hrs. No children under
14 allowed in mine. Write for map
and more information.

Rainbow Lode Mining Claim, King Koenig, Amethyst, aqua-
Box 561, 1220 22nd St., S.W., Love- marine, chryso-
land, CO 80537. Phone (303) 669-   prase, chalcedony,
2589. Open May to snowfall. Other   quartz crystals,

times by appt. Fees: $10/day.   rose quartz,
Free camping.   moonstone
**The Devil's Hole Mine. The Tezak   Rose quartz
brothers, Texas Creek Cafe, Texas
Creek, CO. Fee: $2.00. Obtain
permit at cafe.

CONNECTICUT

Cinque Quarry. Mrs. Rose Cinque, 505   Smoky quartz,
Laurel St., East Haven, CT. Phone   amethyst, dog-
(203) 467-2472. Open 7 AM-5 PM.   tooth calcite
Fee: $2.00 each.
**Gillette Quarry, Haddon Neck, CT.   Minerals
**Borodonaro Mine, Portland, CT 06480.   Feldspar, garnet,
     pyrite, mica,
     quartz
**Branchville Quarry, off Mountain Road,   Phosphate and
Redding, CT. Mr. Mike de Luca, 448   lithium minerals
Limestone Rd., Ridgefield, CT 06877.
Phone (203) 227-7253. Fee: $2.00
each, $50.00 minimum.
**Roxbury Garnet Mine, Mr. Green, Per-   Garnet, stauro-
kins Road, Roxbury, CT. Fee: lite
$1.00/car.
**Roxbury Iron Mine, Mr. Wilber R. Shook,
Painter Hill Road, Roxbury, CT
06783. Write for permission.

FLORIDA

**Newport, FL. Write Buckeye Cellulose   Wacissa (agatized)
Corp., Perry, FL 32347 for permit   coral
application and maps. Fee: $5.00
for 5 days. No charge for under
14 or over 65, but must have permit.

GEORGIA

Staurolite Minerals & Mines. Mr. Oscar   Staurolite, gold,
Robertson, Box 62, Ball Ground, GA   garnet, agate,
30107. Phone (404) 735-3771. Fee: jasper, geodes,
$25/couple. Free camping; free rock   rutile, calcite
museum. Call or write for a reser-
vation.
**Donald Hackney, Blue Ridge, GA. Open   Staurolite "fairy
all year, 8 AM-5 PM. Fee: $2.00 or   crosses," gold,
$3.00/car.   hornblende
Roper Garnet Mine. Mrs. J. Roper, Mgr.   Rhodolite garnet,
Rt. 2, Box 313, Canon, GA 30520.   corundum, beryl
Phone (404) 356-8560. Open May 1

to Oct. 30, 9 AM-5 PM. By appt. in
April for groups. Fee: $3.00 each.
Open every day.

KOA Beryl Mines, Rt. 1, Commerce, GA   Beryl (aquamarine),
  30529. Mr. Wyman Barrineau, phone   garnet, tourmaline
  (404) 335-5535. Open all year.
  Fee: $3 each or $3/couple if regis.
  at campground. Camping $5 for 2 +
  75¢ each over 2. Sewer hookup 50¢.
Crisson Gold Mining Co., Inc. John W.   Gold panning
  Crisson, Rt. 3, Box 317, Dahlonega,
  GA 30533. Phone (404) 864-6366 [of-
  fice] or 864-6368 [home]. Open April 15 to Nov. 1, 10 AM-6 PM. Fee:
  $1.00. Rock and gift shop.
Gold Hills of Dahlonega, Box 487, Dah-   Gold panning
  lonega, GA 30533. Phone (404) 522-
  9563. Open weekends only in April,
  May, Nov. Open daily June to Oct.
  Fee: $1.75; Children $1.50.
Blackburn State Park, Rt. 3 -- Auraria, Gold panning
  Dawsonville, GA 30534. Phone (404)
  864-3789. Panning summer & fall
  (park is open all year). $1 fee
  includes pan rental. Instruction by
  park personnel. Camping, $2.50/
  night. Electricity, bathrooms,
  showers.
**Oconee Springs Quartz. Jane Manly,   Quartz crystals
  Rt. 3, Eatonton, GA 31024.
**Mr. Alton Hayes, Maysville, GA.   Quartz
**J. B. Ivy Farm, RFD, Warrenton, GA   Amethyst
  30828.

HAWAII

**A-AA Affiliates, 132 Kuliouou Rd.,   Field trips
  Honolulu, HI 96821.

IDAHO

**Doney's Rocks & Gems. Mr. Ronald D.   Jasper
  Doney, 106 W. 38 St., Boise, ID
  83704. Phone (208) 344-9133.
**Shorty's Diggins, Box 25, Emerald   Star garnet
  Creek, Fernwood, ID 83830. May 10
  to Oct. 1, 7 days a week. Fee:
  $3.00/day.
Jeppesen Wilson Mining Co., Rt. 2, Box   Opal
  156, Idaho Falls, ID 83401. May 27
  to Nov. 20, 8:30 AM- 4:30 PM. Fees:

$15/day; 8 to 12 yrs. old, $7.50;
non-diggers $1.00.

PoGoCo Mining Co., Mr. Paul DesFosses,
Box 4283, Pocatello, ID 83201.
Phone (208) 232-0110. Free brochure. Fees: $10/day/person; $25/
day/family. Limit of 50 lbs./per-
son. Open every day, June 21 to
Sept. 7. Reservations needed for
weekdays. Camping for self-contained units.

Variscite (crys-
tal and glassy),
turquoise family
of minerals

Emerald Creek Garnet Area, District
Ranger, P.O. Box 407, St. Maries,
ID 83861. Phone (208) 245-2531.
June 1 - Sept. 30, 8 AM-7 PM. Fee:
$4.00. Limit 5 lbs./day, up to 6
days a year. Camping $2.00. Write
for brochure with map and details.

Star garnet

Carol's Rock Shop. John or Carol
Cantlin, P.O. Box 1148, 1901 E.
Main St., Salmon, ID 83467. Phone
(208) 756-4654. May 1 to Sept.,
weather permitting. Fee: $125.00/
day/digger. Includes full-time
guide, food, transportation, tools,
for one to three day trips to areas,
including motel or camping.

Opal (green and
blue), garnets,
quartz, fossils,
petrified wood,
bloodstone, agate,
gold panning

Spencer Opal Mines. May 15-Oct. 1:
Box 113, Spencer, ID 83446. Oct. 1-
May 15: 1862 Rainier St., Idaho
Falls, ID 83401. Digging May 15-
Oct. 1. Fees: $15/day, up to 20
lbs.; excess $1/lb. 8-12 yrs. old,
$7.50/day. Phones: Spencer (208)
374-5476; Idaho Falls (208) 523-0265.

Opal

ILLINOIS

**Dresden Lakes. Ed Rakoski, Lorenzo
Rd., Morris, IL 60450.

Fossils

IOWA

Butch Lewis, Rt. 1, Bonaparte, Iowa
52620. Phone (319) 592-3221. Open
all year. Guide service. No fee;
trading only. Camping nearby;
nominal fees.

Geodes, honeycomb
coral, petrified
wood

**Geode State Park, New London, Iowa.

Geodes

MAINE

Bumpus Mine, <u>Bethel</u>. Mr. Albert Kimball, Box 6, West Bethel, ME 02486. Phone (207) 824-2628. Fees: $2.00/ person; ages 5 to 10, $1.00; under 5 free. Camping $2.00/night. Mine is on Rts. 5 & 35 S. of Bethel.	Beryl, garnet, rose quartz, smoky quartz
Bennett Quarry. See Mrs. Bennett on Lincoln St., <u>Buckfield</u>, ME (down the road about 3 1/2 mi. from Mt. Mica mine, in Paris Hill). Fee: $2.00.	Beryl, tourmaline, rose quartz, others
**Camps of Acadia, Box 202, <u>Eagle Lake</u>, ME 04739. Phone (207) 444-5207.	Guide service
Mt. Mica Gems & Minerals. Pay fee to Mr. & Mrs. George Brown, Lincoln St., <u>Paris Hill</u>, ME, to get permit. Fee: $1.50. Children under 12 free. Phone (207) 364-3060. Open mid-April to mid-November.	Tourmaline, beryl, garnet, feldspar, quartz, muscovite
Black Mountain Mine, <u>Rumford</u>, ME. Fee: $2.00.	Francolite, triphylite, vivianite, albite, others
Perham's Maine Mineral Store, Junc. Rts. 26 & 219, <u>West Paris</u>, ME 04289. Phone (207) 674-2341. No fees. Open weather permitting. Maps to 11 mines available free at store, including Mt. Mica and Bennett Quarry, above. Museum in store; no admission charge. Stop here first, if possible, before going to mines.	Apatite, tourmaline, garnet, rose and smoky quartz, beryl, many others

MARYLAND

**Nature's Exotics, 10419 Armory Ave., <u>Kensington</u>, MD 20795.	Field trips

MASSACHUSETTS

**Betts Manganese Mine, off Rt. 9, <u>Plainfield</u>, MA. Managed by Mr. & Mrs. Timberlake, on Packard Rd. (Prospect St.), off Rt. 9, the same road the mine is on. Fee: $2.00 per person.	Rhodonite, pyrolusite, pyrite, garnet, others
T. J. Gems, Mr. Thomas J. Sheehan, 116 Winfield St., <u>Worcester</u>, MA 01602. Phone (617) 755-3870. Provides personal guide, tools, boxes and news-	Field trips to local sites

papers for specimens. Guide helps
you collect, and you keep what guide
collects. Fee: $20/day; $35/weekend.

MICHIGAN

**Whelan's Stone & Nature Crafts, Shore-   Field trips
   line Resort, Eagle Harbor, MI 49951.
   Natural Storage Co. Mine, 1200 Judd   Gypsum, selenite,
   Ave., S.W., Grand Rapids, MI 49509.   alabaster
   Phone (616) 241-1619. Fee: $1.50.
   Open M-F, 8:30 AM to 5:30 PM; Sat.
   9:30-4:30. Call ahead for informa-
   tion. Groups by reservation only;
   individuals on limited basis.
   Mr. Richard Whiteman, 1439 Garden St.,   Native copper,
   Hancock, MI 49930. Phone (906)   zeolites, agate,
   482-8447. May to Oct. Make re-   prehnite, mo-
   servations one month in advance.   hawkite, Thomp-
   Fee: $75/day for up to 20 people.   sonite
   Field trip conducting and field
   trip information.

MINNESOTA

**Northland Coin & Gem, Inc., 1107 Clo-   Lake Superior
   quet Ave., Cloquet, MN. Ask for   agates
   directions to agate beds. Also
   sells outright.
   Alley Agate Shop, Inc., Broadway Ave.,   Thomsonite
   Box 816, Grand Marais, MN 55604.
   Phone (301) 384-2970. Memorial Day
   to Sept. 1, 9 AM-6 PM Mon.-Sat.;
   Sun. by appt. Fees: $8 per 1/2 day;
   $15/day. Limit 50 lbs. rough/day.
   No limit on loose nodules. Lower
   rates for clubs, senior citizens.
   Must wear eye protection; tools a-
   vailable. Reserv. req. for groups
   of 6 or more. Primitive campsites.
   Thomsonite Beach Motel, Maurice &   Thomsonite, zeo-
   Tania Feigal, Mile Post 403 1/2,   lites, many others
   Lutsen, MN 55612. Phone (218)
   387-1532. Resort. Best digging
   April-Oct. Free digging for
   guests; $12/day/person for non-
   guests.

MISSOURI

Sheffler's Rock Shop, Alexandria, MO   Keokuk area ge-

63430. 6 mi. S. of Alexandria, Junc. of Hwy. 61. Phone (816) 754-3395. Fee: $10/person for up to 100 lbs. Overrun 10¢/lb.

odes, with quartz, calcite, pyrite, barite, selenite needles

Dian's Rock Shop, Kountry Korner, Rte 1, Box 339, Lake Rd. R.B., Flemington, MO 65650. Phone (417) 282-6461. Write for information. No collecting fees. Camping $2.50 to $3.50/night. Open all year, weather permitting, but the snakes are not out in the spring and fall.

Quartz crystal geodes, fossils, iron pyrite

H. L. Mining, Lincoln, MO 65338. 3 mi. N. of Lincoln on US 65. Write L. Harms, 1804 E. 14th, Sedalia, MO 65301. Phone 816) 826-7872. Open all year, weather permitting. Fee: 15¢/lb.

Mozarkite

**St. Francisville, MO. Write to Geodes, P.O. Box 224, Portage, MI 49081 for information about this mine.

Geodes

MONTANA

Mr. Tom Harmon, Box 78, Crane, MT 59217. Phone (406) 482-2534. Guided Yellowstone River trips, by appt. only. April 1 to Oct. 30. Fee: $35/person/day. No limit on minerals found.

Agate, petrified wood, jasper, fossils

Castles Sapphire Mine, 4363 Hart Dr., Helena, MT 59601. Phone (406) 227-5485. Fee: $25/couple; under 12 free. Rental equipment available. Season May 1-Oct. 15. Free camping; no hook-ups.

Sapphires, garnets

Eldorado Bar Sapphire Mine, Helena, MT. Write for brochure: Pramenko Placers, Inc., 106 Terrace Way, Missoula, MT 59801. Phone (406) 549-6203. Fee: $10/person/day. Under 12 free; over age 65, 25% discount on all fees. Open May 1 to Oct. 31. Tools available. Camping available (various fees).

Sapphires, gold

French Bar Mines. Mr. Ron McLean, 7032 Canyon Ferry Rd., Helena, MT. Phone (406) 475-3380. Open May 1-Oct. 1. Fees: $25.00 for 8 buckets or $20.00 for 4 buckets. Buckets

Sapphire, gold, zircon, garnet

and shovels supplied. No charge
for self-contained camping.
Faceting service available.

Gem Mountain Sapphire Mine, Mr. Dick   Sapphires
Taplin, Box 701, Phillipsburg, MT
59858. Open Memorial Day weekend
to Oct. 1. Fees: $20/person/day;
$30 for husband and wife. Camping
available (no hook-ups); $1.00 fee.

NEVADA

Rainbow Ridge Mine, Denio, NV. From   Fire opal
May 26 to Sept., write to Mr. G. K.
Hodson, Rainbow Ridge Mine, Denio,
NV 89404 for brochure & map. Be-
fore May 26, write to Hodson's of
Scottsdale, 7116 First Ave., Scotts-
dale, AZ 85251. Mine open Memorial
Day to mid-Sept. Closed Wed.
BRING WATER! Fees: $5/day; 8-13
years old, $2.50/day.

Royal Peacock Opal Mine, J. Wilson,   Fire opal, fluo-
Denio, NV 89404. Phone Virgin Val-   rescent opal,
ley # 1. Write for map & brochure.   dendritic opal
Open daily. Fees: $5/person; 8-12
yrs., $2.50; non-diggers $1. Two
trailers available at $12/day; re-
serve in advance.

Mr. L. C. Lambright, 1714 Shoffner   Fire opal, agates
Lane, Fallon, NV 89406. Phone (702)
423-2581. Open June 1 to Aug. 1,
closed Mon. & Tues. Call for reservations. Fee: $10/person/day.
Limit 1 lb. opal + 4 lbs. others.
More may be purchased. No children under 12 at mine. No water at
mine. Free camping.

Little Jo Opal Mine, Mr. & Mrs. Ray   Opal, jasper,
Duffield, P.O. Box 203, Gerlach,   agate
NV 89412. Allow 3 wks. for answer.
Open all year, 7 AM-6 PM. Fees:
$5/day; $4 each in groups over 15
people. Free camping.

**Goldfield Gems, Box 495, Goldfield,   Jasper, apache
NV 89013.   tears

Mr. Carl Hayden, Box 528, Jackpot, NV
89825. Phone (702) 755-2259.
Free map of NE Nevada's gemstone
lodes. (Rockhound's area map.)
Write for one.

NEW HAMPSHIRE

**Beauregard Mine, <u>Alstead</u>, NH. Owner: Minerals
Mr. Maloney in Gilson, NH.

Alger Hill Mine. The Trading Post,   Beryl, aquamarine,
Irene or Leonard Guaraldi, Box 72,   clevelandite,
<u>Grafton</u>, NH 03240. On Riddle Hill   quartz, mica,
Road. Phone (603) 523-4895. Open   uraninite, tourma-
April 1 to Nov. 30, 9 AM-5 PM ON   line, feldspar,
WEEKENDS AND HOLIDAYS! Fee: $2/   pyrite, others
person. Children under 18 must be
accompanied by an adult.

Ruggles Mine, Isinglass Mountain,   Beryl, mica, rose
Route 4, <u>Grafton</u>, NH 03240. Open   & smoky quartz,
weekends May 30 to June 17; daily   amethyst, garnet,
June 17 to 3rd weekend in Oct.   about 150 other
Fees: Adults $2.50; 6-12 yrs. $1;   minerals
under 6 yrs. old free. Mineral/
gift shop.

**Palermo Mine, <u>North</u> Groton, NH.   Phosphate minerals,
Owners: Robert Whitmore & Forrest   apatites
Fogg, Weare, NH 03281. Fee: $2.00.

Beryl Mountain Mineral Shop, Mr. Har-   Beryl, mica, gar-
vey Bailey, Beryl Mtn. Road, <u>South</u>   net, spodumeme,
<u>Acworth</u>, NH 03607. Phone (603)   green fluorite,
835-2236. Map to 10 nearby mines,   fluorescent man-
30¢ (mines are free). Mines open   ganapatite, smoky
April to November.   quartz, tourmaline,
   actinolite, others

Old Crook & Brown Gold Mine Dump. E.   Gold, pyrite,
Foley, R.D. #2, Woodsville, NH   arsenopyrite,
03785. Fee: $2/day/person. No   marcasite
charge for children.

NEW JERSEY

Cape May Point. Mr. Larry Hume, P.O.   "Cape May Diamonds"
Box 320, Cape May Point, NJ 08212.   (quartz), jasper,
Phone (609) 884-7079, 641-3433.   fossil shark teeth,
Sunset Beach at foot of Sunset Blvd. arrowheads
Gift & gem shop open every day early
April to Oct. 31st, weekends in Nov.
Free collecting; open to public.

Trotter Mineral Dump, Scott Rd.,   Fluorescents,
R.F.D. #1, Box 54, <u>Franklin</u>, NJ   franklinite, cal-
07416. Manager, Mr. N. Zipco;   cite, magnetite,
phone (201) 827-7327. Open every   <u>300</u> others
day, 9-4. Will open on call if
found closed. Fee: $2/person, 50
lb. limit. Under 10 yrs. old, $1
(with 20 lb./day limit). Bring

UV light. Shop, bathrooms, shed
with AC outlets for checking rocks
with your UV light.

NEW MEXICO

**Sweet Ranch, <u>Cerrillos</u>, NM 87010.   Petrified wood

Deming Agate Shop, Mrs. Emma Lou Lind-   Vein agate; plume,
berg, Rte 2, Box 331, <u>Deming</u>, NM   moss, fortification
88030. Phone (505) 546-9659. Open   agate; nodules, ge-
all year. Has 6 places to dig. Fee   odes, picture sand-
from 10¢-25¢/lb., depending on lo-   stone, others
cation. Free camping.

Deming Enterprises, Mr. Joe Tavernier,   Agate
Rte 2, Box 292, <u>Deming</u>, NM 88030.
Phone (505) 546-7241. Shop is 8 mi.
E. of Deming on State Road 549. O-
pen all year. Fees: 25¢/lb. while
bulldozing; 15¢/lb. other times.

Rock Hound State Park. Write Mr.   Amethyst, opal,
Frank A. Pena, Park Supt., Rock   geodes, agates
Hound State Park, New Mexico State
Park & Recreations Commission,
<u>Deming</u>, NM 88030 for details.

Nitt Mine & Graphic Mine Dumps, Mr.   Azurite, calcite,
William Dobson, Box 141, <u>Magdalena</u>,   allophane, mala-
NM 87825. Phone (505) 854-2236.   chite, smithsonite,
Call first before going. Open all   others
year except mid-Nov. (hunting season) and when it snows. Fee: $2;
20 lb. limit/person. Free camping.

Rainbow Marble Mine. Mr. O. W. Preece,   Marble, agate,
Box 48, <u>Radium Springs</u>, NM 88054.   petrified wood
Phone (505) 526-2181. Open all
year. Fee: $3 for 30 lbs.; 10¢/lb.
over that.

NEW YORK

Diamond Acres, Stone Arabia Road,   Herkimer Diamonds
<u>Fonda</u>, NY. Write F. Hastings, R.D.   (quartz crystals),
#1, Route 30A, Johnstown, NY 12095.   calcite, dolomite
Fee (13 yrs. to adult): $1. Camp-
ing available.

Ace of Diamonds Mine, Rt. 28, <u>Middle-</u>   Herkimer Diamonds
<u>ville</u>, NY 13406. Phone (315) 891-
3622. Open early spring through
late fall, daylight to dark. Fee:
$2/person. Camping fee: $4.50/
night. Brochure available.

Herkimer Diamond Development Corp.,   Herkimer Diamonds
Box 434, <u>Middleville</u>, NY 13406.
Phone (315) 891-7355. On Rt. 28,
7 mi. N. of Herkimer. April 15 to
Nov. 30, 7 days a week, 7 AM-dark.
Fees: $3/adult; $1.50/child under
14. Camping fees: $7 for 2 people.
$1 for each additional person over
3 yrs. old. Mineral museum.

**Old City Diamond Area, Old City Road,   Herkimer Diamonds,
<u>Newport</u>, NY.   calcite, fossils

Barton Mines Corp., Gore Mountain,   Garnet, related
<u>North Creek</u>, NY 12853. Last week   minerals
in June to Labor Day. Guided tours
(with collecting), mineral shop,
retail sales.

Crystal Grove Campsite & Diamond Mine,   Herkimer Diamonds
R.D. #1, <u>St. Johnsville</u>, NY 13452.
Phone (518) 568-9980. Fees: $2.50
for up to 4 hours; $3 all day. Un-
der 14 yrs. old free. Camping fee
$2.50/night; $3 with electricity.

Diamond Ledge, Ives Rd. (off Rt. 29),   Herkimer Diamonds,
<u>Salisbury</u>, NY. Owner: Mr. Jim   calcite crystals,
Ives, R.D. #1, Little Falls, NY   dolomite
13365. Phone (315) 429-9293. O-
pen May 10 to Thanksgiving. Fees:
$2.08; camping $2.08. Special club
rates. Picnic area and restrooms.

The Old Stone Farm, Oxbow Road,   Fossils, Herkimer
<u>Theresa</u>, NY 13691. Ms. Jean   Diamonds, Deer
Schultz. Not one mine--a series of   River ostracods,
places to hunt. No fees; go to   Rossie calcites,
her store for directions.   labradorite,
    golden sphalerites

Henry Rudy Farm, R.D. #2, Blooms   Spinel
Corner Road, <u>Warwick</u>, NY 10990.
Phone (914) 986-7806. Fee: $3/
person/day.

NORTH CAROLINA

Ray Mine (on Bolem Creek Rd.). Mr.   Mica, beryl, apa-
E. L. Briggs, Box 801, <u>Burnsville</u>,   tite, garnet,
NC 28714. Phone (704) 682-2131.   columbite, aqua-
Gatekeeper: Mrs. Carrie Bennett,   marine, quartz
(704) 682-2362. Open all year.
Fee: $3/person. Free camping.

Old Pressley Mine. Mrs. June Trant-   Corundum, feld-
ham, Box 181, Rt. 1, <u>Canton</u>, NC   spar, sapphire,
28716. Phone (704) 648-0778, or   ruby

648-2815. Open all year. Fees: Adults $1; children 50¢. Camping.

**Cranberry Iron Mine, <u>Cranberry</u>, NC 28614. Fee: $1.00. — Epidote, garnet, kyanite

Bradley's Ruby Mine, Mr. Charles T. Bradley, 59 Bidwill St., <u>Franklin</u>, NC 28734. Phone (704) 524-2395. Fees: $3 each; under 12, $2. — Rubies (salted), sapphire, moon-stone, garnet

Caler Creek Mine, Ed Brogden, opera-tor. Rt. 28 in Cowee Valley, <u>Franklin</u>, NC 28734. Fee: $3/day, incl. 4 buckets of paydirt; extra buckets 25¢ each. Digging your own paydirt also allowed. — Ruby, sapphire, garnet, related minerals

Cherokee Ruby Mine, Rt. 4, Box 483, Cowee Valley Rd., <u>Franklin</u>, NC 28734. Mr. & Mrs. James E. Nelson, managers. Fee: $3 each; under 12, $1.50. Gravel, $1 for 4 buckets. — Rubies, sapphires, related minerals

Corundum Hill Enterprises, Inc., Box 593, <u>Franklin</u>, NC 28734. On US Hwy. 64E. Mr. Ed Crisp, manager. Open 7 days a week, 8 AM - 5 PM. Fees: $2/day; gravel $1 for 4 buckets. — Ruby, amethyst, sapphire, emerald, topaz

Dale & Demko's Mine, Rt. 4, Box 460, <u>Franklin</u>, NC 28734. Resort motel with mine. From Nov. 1 to May 1, write Ms. M. H. Demko, 4240 Ocean Drive, Lauderdale-by-the-Sea, FL 33308. Mark envelope "private residence." — Ruby, sapphire

4 K's Star Garnet Mine, Rose Creek Road, <u>Franklin</u>, NC 28734. Manag-ers, Mr. & Mrs. R. Kehle. Fee: $2/person; gravel $1 for 6 buckets. Closed Wednesdays. — Star garnet, sapphire, moon-stone

Gibson Ruby Mine, Cowee Valley Rd., <u>Franklin</u>, NC 28734. Manager: Mr. Gibson. Fees: $3/person; children $2. Gravel 25¢ a bucket. Closed Sundays. — Ruby, sapphire

Gregory Ruby Mine, Cowee Valley Rd., <u>Franklin</u>, NC 28734. Owners: Mr. & Mrs. W. R. Gregory, Box 495, Franklin, NC 28734. Open 7 days a week, 9 AM - dusk. Fee: $2 each. Gravel $1 for 5 buckets. — Ruby, sapphire

Holbrook Ruby Mine, Cowee Valley Rd., <u>Franklin</u>, NC 28734. Manager: Mr. W. Holbrook. Open 8 AM - 5 PM, 7 — Ruby, sapphire, garnet

days a week. Fees: Adults $3,
children $2.

Mine	Minerals
Houston Mine, Rose Creek Rd., Frank-lin, NC 28734. Manager: Mr. J. T. Houston. Open 7 days a week, 9 AM to 5 PM. Fee: $2/person. Gravel $1 for 5 buckets.	Sapphire, garnet
Jacobs Ruby Mine, Cowee Valley Rd., Franklin, NC 28734. Manager: Mr. R. Hedden. Open 7 days a week, 8 AM - 5 PM. Fees: Adults $3; children 7-11, $2. Gravel 25¢/bucket.	Ruby, sapphire, garnet
McCook's Rhodolite Mine, Rt. 28N, Franklin, NC 28734. Manager: Mr. L. Fortune. Open 7 days a week, 8 AM - 5 PM. Fees: $2; gravel, 25¢ a bucket. Digging your own gravel OK.	Rhodolite garnet, sapphire
Mason Mountain Rhodolite & Ruby Mine, Brown & Martha Johnson, Hwy. 28 (Bryson City Rd.), Rt. 4, Box 742, Franklin, NC 28734. Phone (704) 524-4570. Fees: $2; children under 12, $1. Manager: Mrs. Pat Campbell.	Rhodolite garnet, kyanite, garnet, moonstone, ruby, sapphire, quartz
Mincy Mine, S.R. 1001, Franklin, NC 28734. Owners: C. Kimmel & Wm. Reynolds. Open 8 AM - 5 PM. Fee: $3; gravel 25¢ a bucket.	Bronze sapphires
Rockhound Haven Mine, Rt. 28N, Frank-lin, NC 28734. Manager: Mr. H. Mor-gan. Open 7 days a week, 8:30 AM-5 PM. Fee: $2; gravel $1 for 6 buckets.	Rhodolite garnet
Sheffield Mine, Cowee Valley Rd., Franklin, NC 28734. Manager: Mr. W. Sheffield. Open 7 days a week, 8 AM - 5 PM. Fees: $3; children $2; gravel 25¢ a bucket.	Ruby, sapphire, garnet
Shuler Ruby Mine, Cowee Valley Rd., Franklin, NC 28734. Owner: Mrs. R. Shuler. Open 8 AM - 5 PM; closed Sundays. Fees: $3; chil-dren $2; gravel 4 buckets for $1.	Ruby, sapphire, garnet
**Tessentee Amethyst Mine, Box 592, Franklin, NC 28734. Fee: $3.00.	Amethyst, garnet
Yukon Mine, Rt. 4, Box 452, Franklin, NC 28734. Grace Donaldson, owner. Phone (704) 524-6186. Open all year. Fees: $3; under 12 yrs. old, $2. Camping $3.	Ruby (salted), garnet, sapphire
**Randleman Amethyst Farm, Iron Station, NC 28080.	Amethyst

Reel Mine, Ruth & Fred Sanders, <u>Iron Station</u>, NC 28080. — Amethyst

Playmore Beach, N.C. Rt. 18. Mr. Charles H. DeVoto, Box 390, Rt. 7, <u>Lenoir</u>, NC 28645. Open 9 AM-sunset. Fee: $2 each. Campground. — Gold panning

North Carolina Mining Museum, P.O. Box 98, <u>Little Switzerland</u>, NC 28749. Phone (704) 765-MINE. Open May 1 to Oct. 31. Fees: $3; students, grades 1 to 12, $2; senior citizens $2. Send for literature. A museum in a real, underground mine. Basic tools and screens furnished. "SALT-ed" Gemstone Mine, nearby, has minerals from various mines in the area (separate fees). "SALT-ed" open Memorial Day to Labor Day. — 36 minerals, incl. amazonite, apatite, aquamarine, mica, feldspar, kyanite, garnet, etc.

Reed Gold Mine, <u>Locust</u>, NC. Owned by the state. Open March to Oct., Tues.-Sat. 9-5, Sun. 1-5. Phone (704) 786-8337. Fee: $3, with two pans of ore. Film & exhibit at visitors' center. Guided tour of restored underground workings. — Gold panning

Bettis Brothers Farm. Cleve & Jeff Bettis, Box 259, <u>Marble</u>, NC 28905. Open all year. Fee: $2/person/day. — Staurolite

Troy Watson, Rt. 3, Box 144, <u>Newland</u>, NC 28657. Mine is on Henson Creek Rd. All equipment furnished. Open 9 AM - 5 PM; closed Sundays. Fee: $3/person. — Beryl: green, blue, golden. Garnet: black, red. Aquamarine.

Cotton Patch Mine, <u>New London</u>, NC 28127. Mr. Glenn Nance. Phone (704) 463-5797. Open March 1 to Oct. 31, 8 AM-6 PM. Fee: $5, incl. 4 pails of ore, use of pan, and instructions. Camping $5/day; light & water hook-ups, showers, restrooms, snack bar. — Gold panning

**Bill Burleson's Moonstone Mine. 2.5 mi. North of Plumtree on Roaring Creek Rd., <u>Spruce Pine</u>, NC 28777. — Moonstone

OHIO

Nethers Farm, Mr. John Nethers, 3680 Flint Ridge Road, <u>Hopewell</u>, OH 43746. Phone (614) 787-2263. Open all year, weather permitting. Fee: — Flint; clear, rose, and smoky quartz; chalcedony in flint

$2 per person for up to 20 lbs.
25¢ a pound over that.

**Basil Norris, Rt. 2, Pert Mill Road, Nashport, OH 43830. Fee: $1.	Flint
Nellie Blue-Black Flint. Write Mr. A. Clarke, Box 115, Warsaw, OH 43844. Mine is in Nellie, OH. Mr. R. E. Davidson, R.D. # 3, Warsaw, OH 43844, serves as a collecting guide at the Clarke farm. Fee: $1.25.	Agate, flint
Mason's House of Flint. Clayton & Evelyn Mason, 15886 Flint Ridge Rd. S.E., Newark, OH 43055. Phone (614) 787-2503. Open April to mid-Nov. Fee: 5¢/lb. Camping $3.50/day; electric hook-ups, restrooms, and showers.	Flint

OKLAHOMA

Ferguson Ranch. Mr. Donald J. Snider, R. 1, Box 48, Cache, OK 73527. Phone (405) 429-8340 nights & weekends. Open year-round, to groups of 10 or more only. Fee: $2 up to 10 lbs.; 20¢/lb. over that.	Barite crystals, geodes, balls
Roberts Ranch, Mr. M. J. Roberts, Box 72, Kenton, OK 73946. Phone (405) 261-7410. Fees: 25¢/lb. except $2/lb. for coprolite and cycad.	Petrified wood, jasper, rose agate, algae, cycad, coprolite
**Shobert Farm, Noble, OK 73068. Fee: $4/person for 30 lbs.; 50¢/lb. over that.	Barite roses
**Fred Reynold's Rose Rock Farm, Old State No. 9, Norman, OK 73069.	Barite roses

OREGON

Antelope Ranch, Harry & Nadine Armstrong, Box 79, Antelope, OR 97001. Phone (503) 489-3350. Open all year, weather permitting. Fee: 25¢/lb.; $3 minimum. Free camping for self-contained vehicles.	Thundereggs, nodules, jasper, quartz crystal geodes, moss agate
Eagle Valley Ranch, Don & Candy Gomes, P.O. Bin 6A, Antelope, OR 97001. Phone (503) 489-3318. Open all year, weather permitting. Fees: from 20¢ to 50¢ a pound. Free camping.	Moss & blue agate, petrified wood, geodes with calcite and amethyst

**Bedortha Ranch, <u>Ashwood</u>, OR 97711.   Petrified wood
**Evans Ranch, <u>Ashwood</u>, OR 97711.   Agate
   Friend's Ranch, Mr. Darrell Friend,   Thundereggs
     Box 41, <u>Ashwood</u>, OR 97711. Phone
     (503) 489-3252. Open May-Oct., 9
     AM-5 PM. Fee: 35¢/lb.
   Keegan Ranch, Box 11, <u>Ashwood</u>, OR   Bull's-eye tube
     97711. Phone (503) 489-3294, or   agate, sometimes
     546-2953. Call before going, if   with plumes;
     possible. Open March-Nov. Fees: jasper; amethyst;
     from 35¢ to $1.00 a pound. Free   Keeganite
     camping; outside bathrooms; water.
   The David McDonald Ranch, Ms. Lisa   Petrified wood,
     McDonald, Box 35, <u>Ashwood</u>, OR   limb casts, blue
     97711. Phone (503) 489-3344. Open   agate, thundereggs
     May 1 to Oct. 31. Fee: 50¢/lb.
**Marston's Petrified Wood Ranch, Ash-   Petrified wood
   <u>wood</u>, OR 97711. Fee: 50¢/lb.
   Swanson Agate & Egg Beds. Mrs. Ger-   Thundereggs; pet-
     ald Thornton, Box 16, <u>Ashwood</u>, OR   rified wood; polka
     97711. Phone (503) 489-3259.   dot, red moss,
     Fees: 25¢ to 50¢ a lb. Open May-   Paulina, or gold
     Oct. Bring hard rock digging   agates
     tools. Camping avail.; well water.
   Triangle Cross Ranch. See Sandy Sym-   Green moss agate
     mons, Main St., <u>Ashwood</u>, OR 97711.
     Phone (503) 489-3293. Open April
     1 to Nov. 1, weather permitting.
     Fee: 50¢/lb. Camping at Ashwood
     Grange, for a donation.
   Clyde Thissell Ranch, Box 218, <u>Burns</u>,   Snake agate
     OR 97220. Fee: $2 each for up to   (chalcedony)
     6 lbs.; 40¢/lb. over that.
   King Solomon's Surprise Mine, <u>Grant's</u>   Gold, native mer-
     <u>Pass</u>, OR. Owner: Mr. T. H. Bohm-   cury, cinnabar,
     ker, Gold Panning Safaris, 1413   native copper,
     N.W. 9th St., Corvallis, OR 97330.   josephinite,
     Phone (503) 745-5113. Open April   platinum, spinel
     to Oct. Fee: $65 for two days, in-
     cluding use of tents and tools,
     and food.
**Burnett's Agate Beds, <u>Lebanon</u>, OR   Agate, carnelian
   97355.
   Drummond's Agate Beds, 37290 Rock Hill   Carnelian, jasper
     Dr., <u>Lebanon</u>, OR 97355. Phone
     (503) 258-3246. Write for map. O-
     pen May-Sept., 7 AM-5 PM. Fee: $5
     (no limit on rock). Camping $2 a
     night with digging fee; others $3.

Hay Creek Ranch, Ashwood Star Route, <u>Madras</u>, OR 97741. Ms. Clarene Aitken, Mgr. Phone (503) 475-3789. 12 mi. E. of Madras on B St. Open April to Nov.; other months by appt. Guide available. Fees: $3/person, up to 20 lbs. each. Overnight camping; no water.
 Hay Creek blue agate, thundereggs, jasper, petrified wood

Pony Creek Digs. Maxine Grosse, Box 348, <u>Madras</u>, OR 97741. Shop is 17 mi. N. of Madras on Hwy. 97. Phone (503) 489-3322. Open Apr. 1 - Nov. 15. About 24 agate beds leased from ranches in the area. Fees: 50¢ to $1.00/lb.
 Petrified wood, thundereggs, agate, jasper

Johnnie Richardson's Kennedy Ranch & Priday Agate Beds. Gateway Route Box 440, <u>Madras</u>, OR 97741. Phone (503) 475-2680. 13 mi. NW of Madras. Open all year, weather permitting. Hard rock mining equipment needed. Fee: 20¢/lb.; no minimum. Free camping; no hookups. Free showers at shop.
 Red, yellow, purple moss agate; polka dot agate; Priday thundereggs; petrified wood

Lucky Strike Thunderegg Mine. Mr. Leonard Kopcinski, Box 128, <u>Mitchell</u>, OR 97750. Open 8 AM-6 PM. Write for map & directions. Fee: 35¢/lb.; minimum $3 per car.
 Thundereggs, picture jasper

Mr. James Wood, Box 45, Arago Route, <u>Myrtle Point</u>, OR 97458. Jade claim in Siskiyou National Forest. Fee: $3.00.
 Jade

Mansfield of Rock, Ms. Margaret Mansfield, Box 147, <u>New Pine Creek</u>, OR 97635. Phone (916) 946-4101. Season approx. June 20-Oct. 15. Fees "by the pound." Free camping. Has about 8 different mines.
 Obsidian: pink, blue, purple, green, spiderweb, rainbow

Crook County Chamber of Commerce, Box 546, <u>Prineville</u>, OR 97754. Phone (503) 447-6304. Write for map of places to dig. No fee for map or for digging. Open "when the roads are good."
 Agate, others

Prospect Mtn. Mining & Mfg., 36741 Zeleny Rd., <u>Scio</u>, OR 97374. Mr. A. G. Zeleny. Phone (503) 394-2403. Open all year, weather permitting. Fees: $5/day up to 25 lbs.; 25¢/lb. over that. Dry camping in summer
 Petrified (agatized) wood

for self-contained units.

Oran & Mildred Belveal, 26137 Old
Holley Rd., Sweet Home, OR 97386.
Phone 367-5985. Open all year.
Fee: $2.50/day. Free camping; rest
room and water.
  Petrified wood,
agate

**J. J. Macker Ranch, Holley Rt., Sweet
Home, OR 97386.
  Petrified wood

**Clear Creek (Vernonia), OR. Bring
rubber boots & digging equipment.
$1 or $2 donation per car suggested.
  Carnelian, plume
and other agate

Priday Polka Dot Agate, Willowdale,
OR. Write Dr. Eugene Winter,
Prof's Rock Shop, 56 N. College
Ave., College Place, WA 99324.
Phone (509) 527-2282. Open June-
Sept. by appt., or contact Sandy's
Rock Shop, Ashwood, OR. Closed
Sat. Fee: 10¢ to $1/lb., depend-
ing on quantity and quality.
  Agate, jasper

PENNSYLVANIA

Pequea Silver Mines, R.D. 1, Conesto-
ga, PA 17516. Phone [mine] (717)
872-6592; [office] 393-5611. Mr.
Howard S. Bunting, P.O. Box 622,
Lancaster, PA 17604. Open Memorial
Day to Sept., 10 AM-6 PM. Closed
Mondays. Winter hours by appt. only, 1 week ahead. Fees: mine tour,
$1; rockhounding, $3; rockhounding
tour, $5. Camping with water, elec-
tricity, and dump station.
  Limestone, quartz,
galena (silver-
bearing), margarite,
rutile, soapstone,
talc, serpentine

**Bigham Mine. Mr. Stanley Pitts,
Greenstone-Iron Springs Rd., Green-
stone, PA.
  Copper minerals,
epidote, quartz

**Henry T. Levi, 103 Prospect St.,
Nanticoke, PA 18634. Phone (717)
735-1493. Information on coal
mines in Ashley, Mountain Top,
Nanticoke.
  Coal

Kibblehouse Quarry, Perkiomenville,
PA. Open 8 AM-3:30 PM; Sat. 8 AM-
11:30 AM. Release must be signed
in office. Hard hats, goggles,
hard-toed footwear must be worn.
No collecting during or just after
heavy rain. No fees.
  Minerals

French Creek Mines, St. Peter's, PA
19470. Owner: Mr. Peter Chonka.
  Magnetite, calcite,
hematite, chalco-

Phone (215) 469-6140. Mine is
behind house; ask in town for
directions to house. Fee: $2; un-
der 16 years old, 50¢.

pyrite, azurite,
pyrite, others

SOUTH DAKOTA

**Mr. Louis Stratton, Box 695, Custer,
SD 57730. Guide.

Minerals

Black Hills Expeditions, Inc., Mr.
Edward D. Baier, Box 206, Ft.
Meade, SD 57741. Phone (605) 347-
4129. Guided trips on weekends.
Fee of $100.00 per vehicle includes
detailed map, so you can return in
future years at no additional cost.

Gold panning,
Fairburn & other
agates, jasper,
petrified wood,
fossils

**Flying U Ranch, Bradfields, Kodoka, SD
57543.

Agate, petrified
wood

**Big Foot Ranch, Porcupine, SD 57772.

Chalcedony, fossils

**Black Hills Minerals, Skyline Drive,
Keystone Rt., Box 4, Rapid City,
SD 57701.

Information, group
guide

Fairburn Agate Beds. Black Hills
Showcase Gems & Minerals, Box 8815,
Keystone Rt., Rapid City, SD 57701.
Phone (605) 342-7847. About 1000
sq. miles of agate beds. Open all
year. No fees. Campground at
agate beds (free). Write for more
details.

Fairburn agates,
agatized wood,
floral jasper,
moss agate, tubu-
lar coral, fossils
(several types)

TENNESSEE

Betty & Elmer Yocum, Rt. 9, Box 115B,
Sparta, TN 38583. Phone (615) 738-
8162. Open April-Nov. Fees: $2
each up to 10 lbs. of agate; 25¢ a
lb. over that.

Calfkiller agate,
jasper, quartz
crystals

Jack Silvertooth, Rte. 2, Box 250,
Wartrace, TN 37183. Phone (615)
389-6165. Open all year. Call or
write ahead to be sure he is home.
Fee: $3 or 30¢/lb., whichever is
higher. Free camping; no hook-ups.

Carnelian, agate,
crinoids, coral

TEXAS

**Anderson Ranch, Alpine, TX 79830.

Agate

**Aqua Frio Ranch, c/o B. P. McKinney,
Alpine, TX 79830.

Agate, petrified
wood

**Henderson Ranch, Alpine, TX 79830.

Agate

**Maverick Mt. Rock Shop, Terlingua   Field trips
   Rt. Box 390, <u>Alpine</u>, TX 79830.
**Roadrunner Park, <u>Alpine</u>, TX 79830.   Guides
**Mr. Earl Rudder, State Highway 118,   Petrified wood,
   <u>Alpine</u>, TX 79830. Fee: $10.00.   agate
  Stillwell Ranch, Mrs. Hallie Still-   Agates, jasper,
   well, Box 430, Big Bend, <u>Alpine</u>,   petrified wood
   TX 79830. Phone (915) 376-2244.
   Open all year. Fee: 50¢/lb.
   Trailer park, camping; all facil-
   ities, store, ice, restrooms,
   showers, phone, T.V. hook-ups.
  Woodward Ranch, Mr. J. F. Woodward,   Plume, pompom,
   Box 40, Terlingua Rt., <u>Alpine</u>, TX   pastel bouquet
   79830. Phone (915) 364-2271. Open   agates; bloodstone,
   all year. 16 mi. S. of Alpine on   carnelian, fire
   State Hwy. 118. Three ranches: opal
   "Red Plume," "Pom Pom," and "Pastel Bouquet" agates. Fees: $3/
   person/day, up to 25 lbs.; 25¢ a
   lb. over that. Trailer park or
   free camping.
**Erdman Ranch (Mamie Erdman), <u>Falls</u>   Agatized wood,
   <u>City</u>, TX 78113. Guided field   palm, cycads
   trips for a fee. Write first.
**Mr. & Mrs. Tessman, Farm Road 1344,   Golden petrified
   <u>Falls City</u>, TX 78113.   palm wood
**Singing Hills Ranch, <u>Laredo</u>, TX 78040.   Agate
**Hall Ranch, Mrs. Anna Hall, 110   Minerals
   Marble, <u>Llano</u>, TX 78643.
  ME Ranch Co., E. K. Beanland, P.O.   Agates: black,
   Box 745, <u>Marfa</u>, TX 79843. Phone   bouquet, pastel,
   (915) 729-4141. Now administered   banded; opal
   by Mr. Woodward (see Woodward
   Ranch, above). Open all year except Nov. Fee: $15 for up to 30
   lbs.; 50¢/lb. over that. Free
   camping: water available; no
   facilities.
  Mountain View Rock Shop (Mr. Paul   Agate: bouquet &
   Wofford), P.O. Box 603, <u>Marfa</u>, TX   black plume; moss
   79843. Phone (915) 729-4028.   agate; jasper;
   Guide with 200 sections to hunt on.   petrified wood
   Fees: Under 10 in party, $15 each;
   over 10 in party, $12.50 each. Up
   to 35 lbs. of rock included. Over
   that, 35¢/lb.
  Wayne Hoffman, <u>Mason</u>, TX. Mrs. Wes   White & blue topaz,
   Loeffler [has the key], Menard   smoky quartz
   Route, Mason, TX 76856. Phone
   (915) 347-6415. Closed Nov. 16 to

Jan. 1 (deer season). Fees: $5/
day; $3 for clubs with 10 or more
people. Bring digging tools.
Free camping.

Ince Ranch, Mr. & Mrs. Edgar Ince,   Topaz, quartz
Box 411, Mason, TX 76856. Phone
(915) 347-5694. Closed Nov. 15
for deer hunting. Fee: $5 each.

Mr. & Mrs. Roy Priess, F.B.G. Rt.,   Topaz, smoky
Box 3, Mason, TX 76856. Phone (915) quartz
347-6757. Closed Nov. 1 to Jan. 1.
Fee: $4 each. Free camping; no
facilities.

**Schwanke Ranch, Mr. Bob Raspberry,   Topaz
Mason, TX 76856.

Seaquist Honey Creek Ranch, Garner or Blue & clear topaz,
Clara Seaquist, Box 35, 400 Broad   smoky quartz
St., Mason, TX 76856. Phone (915)
347-5431. Bring digging tools.
Closed Nov. 16-Dec. 1 (deer season). Fee: $5/person/day. Camp-
ing $3/day; with electricity, $6.

**Matejowski's Bluebonnet Farm, Mr. Mar- Petrified wood,
vin Matejowski, Rt. 1, Box 196,   incl. palm wood
Nechanitz, TX. Fee: $1/person/day,
for up to 20 lbs.; 20¢/lb. over
that. Palm wood, $1/lb. Free
camping.

Lambert Ranch, C. B. & Sarah Lambert, Limestone, fossils,
Rt. 1, Box 127, San Saba, TX 76877. crinoid stems,
Phone (915) 372-5042. Closed for   opalized coral
deer hunting Nov. 15-Jan. 1. Fee:
$2/person, up to 30 lbs. Camping
allowed.

Mother Lode Ranch, Mr. & Mrs. H. D.   Petrified wood,
House, 1911 Mesquite, Three Rivers, incl. palm wood,
TX 78071. Phone (512) 786-2681.   fern buds·
Open Jan. 1 to Nov. 10. Fee: $5
per vehicle.

Bob's Knob, Box 849, Falcon Reservoir, Rio Grande agate
Zapata, TX 78076. Mr. Bob Sadler.
Open all year. Rock hunting is not
as good in the winter, when the
lake is high. Camping.

Falcon Rock & Jewelry Shop, Mrs. Char- Agates, jasper,
leen Deaton Melton, P.O. Box 464, petrified wood
Zapata, TX 78076. Phone (512) 765-
4455. "Ramirez Ranch," open Oct. 1
to May. Fee: $3/person. Shop open
Oct. 1 to May 1, 10 AM-6 PM; closed
Fri. & Sun. mornings.

Johnny's Rock Shop, Hiway 89, <u>Elsi-nore</u>, UT 84724. Phone (801) 527-4096. Reservations suggested. Fee: 30¢/lb. Camping permitted. — Clay canyon agate

**Nephi Onyx Mine. Mr. Dale N. Stevens, Steve's Stone, Rock, Lumber and Wood Yard, Star Rt., <u>Jensen</u>, UT 84035. — Onyx

Red Horn Coral Mine, G. L. or Donna Odekirk, 4594 West 5415 So., <u>Kearns</u>, UT 84118. Phone (801) 966-5481. Open Aug. 1 to Oct. 15. Write for maps. Fee: $5/lb. Free camping. — Red horn coral, jasper, fossils

**McDonald Opal, Hwy. 257 North, <u>Mil-ford</u>, UT. Fee: $10 for 10 lbs. One fee pays for entire immediate family. — Fire opal; bubble, bacon, sagenite, and plume agates

VERMONT

Vermont Asbestos Group (VAG), <u>Edén Mills</u>, VT. Take Rt. 100 to Eden Mills; the mine is north of the village. Operators dump rock outside of mine gate for collectors. — Serpentine, idocrase, magnetite, others

VIRGINIA

Dobins Prospect & Morefield Mine, Mr. Deck R. Boyles, Rt. 4, Box 307, <u>Amelia</u>, VA 23002. Phone (804) 561-2395. Open all year. Fee: $1 per person at each mine. — Beryl, amazonite, topaz, others

Ligon Mine, State 651. Mr. Kenneth A. Hooley, Rt. 4, Box 158, <u>Amelia</u>, VA 23002. Phone (804) 561-3067. Open all year. Fee: $2. — Rose & clear quartz, mica books, beryl, tourmaline, feldspar

Rutherford Mine. Mr. Crawford Keener, <u>Amelia</u>, VA 23002. Open all week. Fee: $1; 6-12 years old, 50¢. — Amazonite, moonstone, garnet

CLOSED   CLOSED

Amherst Amethyst Mine. Mrs. Mary L. Schaar, Rt. 2, <u>Amherst</u>, VA 24521. Call or write first to be sure someone is home. Fee: $4/person/day. — Amethyst, quartz

Harris Mica Mine Farm, Mrs. Owen Harris, Rt. 2, Box 137, <u>Beaver Dam</u>, VA 23015. Phone 449-6216. Fee: $1/person. Camping, $2/night; no electricity. — Moonstone, garnet, quartz, mica, kyanite, amazonite

**Dixie Rhodonite Mine. Mr. Michael
Landes, Dixie Rock Shop, P.O. Box
177, Fork Union, VA 23055. Mining
by appointment only, one month in
advance. Minimum fee, $200.00.
Write for information.
Rhodonite, rhodo-
chrosite, magnetit

**Brickhill Farm, Goldvein, VA 22720.
Gold

**Luck Quarry, State Rt. 7, Leesburg,
VA 22075. Fee: $1.
Prehnite

Clark & Haynes Union 76 Service Station, Rt. 57, Martinsville, VA.
No fee.
"Fairy stones"
(staurolite)

Fairy Stone State Park, Martinsville,
VA. Stones are found at southern
tip of park near State 57, at Pat-
rick & Henry county line. No fees.
"Fairy stones"

WASHINGTON

Frank & Ollie's Rock & Gem Shop, Ward
& Barbara Lynch, owners. 123 First
Ave., Okanogan, WA 98840. Phone
422-3730. Field trips; write for
details.
Serpentine, blue
agate, thulite,
rose quartz, aven-
turine, others

**Mr. Glen Coby, Old Hard Rock Bennet
Diggings, Vernita Star Rt., Sunny-
side, WA 98944. Fee: $1.
Petrified wood (?)

Silver Dollar Cafe, Vernita Star Rt.,
Sunnyside, WA 98944. Ask for direc-
tions at the cafe.
Petrified wood

Northwest Gem Co., 3841 6th Ave.,
Tacoma, WA 98406. Phone (206) 752-
8342. Rock & relic guided tours,
Yukon to Costa Rica. Write for
brochure.
Rocks, minerals,
crystals, gems,
artifacts

Ginkgo Petrified Forest State Park,
Vantage, WA, and other locations.
25 lb./person/day limit on state
land. Bring water. No fees.
Write to Washington State Dept. of
Game, Lt. Murry Wildlife Rec. Area,
14th & B St., Ellensburg, WA 98926
for information on free collecting
on state game land.
Petrified wood,
common opal

WEST VIRGINIA

**Tyler Mt. Lapidary, 5257 Big Tyler
Rd., Charleston, WV 25512.
Field trip
information

WISCONSIN

**House of Suzanne, 430 East Grand Ave.,
   Wisconsin Rapids, WI 54494.

Free map of central
Wisconsin mineral
locations

WYOMING

Buck Rogers Empress Gems, P.O. Box 53,
   Jeffrey City, WY 82310. Phone
   (307) 544-2532. Winter: 795 Garfield, Lander, WY 82520. Phone
   (307) 332-5513. Conducts gem hunts
   from May to Oct. Reservations required. Fee: $15 1st day; $12 2nd
   day; $10 after that. Free camping.

Fossils, jade,
agate, quartz,
petrified wood,
jasper, serpentine,
others

Dryhead Agate Diggings, 35 mi. N. of
   Lovell, Wyoming, on Hwy. #37. Dryhead Agate Co., 1601 Bitterroot Dr.,
   Billings, MT 59101. Phone (406)
   259-1329 (Mr. Gene Frates). Mine
   is open June 1 to Oct. 1. Permit
   can be obtained at mine. Write to
   Montana for map & more details.
   Fee: $15/day/person. Dry camp &
   restroom; no fee for camping. Pick,
   shovel, and bar needed for digging.

Dryhead agate

**Mr. Lewis ("Hop") Vondrasek, Muddy
   Gap, WY. He will guide you to his
   claims for a fee. Write first!

Jade, Wiggins &
Dobois woods,
agates

Warfield Fossil Quarries, Inc., Mr.
   Rick Hebdon, Star Rt., Box 7,
   Thayne, WY 83127. Open June 1-
   Sept. 1. Write for brochure & map.
   Fees: $18/day for 1-2 persons;
   $15/day for 4-5 persons; $12/day
   for 6 and over. Camping available;
   no hook-ups.

Fossil fish

CANADIAN DIGGING SITES

DIGGING SITES ARE ARRANGED BY PROVINCES, AND THEN BY TOWNS
WHERE THE MINES ARE LOCATED (UNDERLINED), IN ALPHABETICAL
ORDER. SEE INTRODUCTION FOR THE MEANING OF THE ** SYMBOL.

DIGGING SITE	MINERALS

ONTARIO

**Princess Sodalite Mine (Hwy. 500,
CLOSED 2 1/2 mi. E. of town), P.O. Box
84, Bancroft, Ontario, Canada
KOL 1C0. Phone (613) 332-3337.
Fee: 50¢/lb. for sodalite.

Blue sodalite,
green apatite, cal-
cite, sunstone

**Albert Berger Farm, Germanicus Road,
Eganville, Ontario, Canada. Fee:
50¢/lb.

Apple-green ama-
zonite

**Timber Trails Resort Campground, R.R.
1, Pass Lake P.O., Ontario, Canada.
Phone: Pass Lake 5561. 20 mi. E.
of Thunder Bay on Hwy. 17.

Rock hunting

**Diamond Willow Mine, Mr. Gunnard
Noyes, Pearl, Ontario, Canada.
Fee: $1/lb.

Amethyst

**Ontario Gem Amethyst Mine, Pearl, On-
tario, Canada. Fee: $1/lb.

Amethyst

Quadeville East Quarry (Lot 23, Beryl
Pit). Fran McCoy, Wal-Gem Lapidary, P.O. Box 43, Quadeville,
Ontario, Canada KOJ 2G0. Phone
(613) 758-2805. Open last week in
May to mid-Oct. Must sign release
at shop. Fees: $5/day/person; 50¢
for children under 12. No extra
charge for rock taken.

Beryl, clear and
smoky quartz,
amazonite, moon-
stone, black tour-
maline, others

Thunder Bay Amethyst Mine Panorama,
div. of Precious Purple Gemstones
Ltd., Mr. S. W. Lukinuk, Box 26,
Thunder Bay, Ontario, Canada P7C
4V5. Phone (807) 622-6413 or
(Mr. Enns) 622-6908. Open mid-
May-mid-Oct., 9:30 AM-7:30 PM.
Fees: $1/person; children under 10
free. $1/lb. & up for amethysts
dug.

Amethyst.

QUEBEC

M. Gérard Adam Mine, M. Gérard Adam,
420, 11e rang, Bonsecours, Québec,

Quartz crystals

Canada JOE 1H0. Phone (514) 535-
6713. Open May to Sept. Prefers
letters in French. If not possible,
call M. Michel Adam at (514) 539-
0640. Fee: $3/hour, but with only
small tools. Camping available.
De-Mix & Poudrette Quarries, <u>St. Hil-</u>
<u>aire</u>, Québec, Canada (20 mi. W. of
Montréal). De-Mix, Inc. & M. Poudrette Co. Open only to clubs
with insurance in effect.

Galena, marcasite,
molybdenite, many
others

SITES NOW CLOSED TO COLLECTORS

In cases where a rock shop is listed, it is usually only the associated digging site that is closed. The shop itself is usually still open.

ARIZONA:
Mine dumps at Bagdad
Greer's Milky Ranch,
  Holbrook
Black Mountain Opal
  Mine, Kingman
ARKANSAS:
Coleman Crystal Mine,
  Jessieville
CALIFORNIA:
Calico Silver Onyx Mine,
  Yermo
Himalaya Mine and dumps
Nowak's Fire Opal Dig-
  gings, San Fernando
COLORADO:
Blue Barite Diggings,
  Stoneham
Crystal Peak & Indian
  Peak
Florissant Gems &
  Minerals
Plume Agate Beds, Del
  Norte
CONNECTICUT:
Walden Mine, Portland
GEORGIA:
Withlacoochee coral,
  Clyattville
Aluminum Silicate
  Corp., Lincolnton
IDAHO:
The Rock Tepe & Tepe
  Mine, Marsing
ILLINOIS:
Shinnybarger Farm,
  Quincy
MARYLAND:
State Line Pits,
  Baltimore
MICHIGAN:
Adventure Mines,
  Greenland

MISSOURI:
Timberline Lake Rock & Gem
  Shop, Lincoln
MONTANA:
Guffey's Sapphire Mine, Helena
Cornish Sapphire Mine,
  Philipsburg
NEVADA:
Quartette Mine, San Clemente
NEW MEXICO:
West Mesa Rock Shop,
  Albuquerque
Blanchard Mine, Bingham
Keith Ranch, Cerrillos
NEW YORK:
Powers Farm, Canton
Molholsky's Diamond Farm,
  Newport
Leib's Moonstone Mine, Saranac
  Lake
NORTH CAROLINA:
Emerald Valley Mines,
  Hiddenite
OHIO:
Neibarger Farm, Hopewell
OREGON:
Whiting's Horse Heaven Ranch,
  Antelope
Big Muddy Ranch, Ashwood
Moore's Agate Beds, Lebanon
Carey Agate Beds, Prineville
PENNSYLVANIA:
Cedar Hill Quarry, Lancaster
  County
Pit II, Mazon Creek Fossils
TENNESSEE:
Mr. Joe G. Arnold, Wartrace
TEXAS:
Charles Moss Ranch, Llano
Brushy Canyon Ranch, Marahon
Joe Bishop, Marfa
UTAH:
Fisher's Rock Shop, Orderville

(continued on next page)

Closed Sites (continued)

VIRGINIA:
Winfree Prospect, Amelia
Bishop Mine Dumps, Lynch Station
Mr. Frank Webb, Martinsville
WASHINGTON:
Adna & Lucas Creek areas
Brown's Ranch, Mattawa
Lanny R. Ream, Mt. Vernon
Agate Beach, Port Angeles
WYOMING:
Gemstone Enjoyment, Casper
Gemco Rock Shop, "Tin Cup Mtn.,"
    Jeffrey City
Glendo Agate Beds, Wheatland
CANADA (ONTARIO):
Ruby Mine, Hardwood Lake
Beryl Point Mine, Quadeville

GENERAL TOURIST INFORMATION

The states listed below will provide literature for
tourists, including maps and information about accommodations, restaurants, special events, and rockhunting. There is no charge for this information,
except where noted.

ALASKA

Division of Geological and Geophysical Surveys, Box
80007, College, AK 99701. Information Circular 18:
"Amateur Gold Prospecting in Alaska."

Department of Commerce and Economic Development,
Division of Tourism, Pouch E, Juneau, AK 99811. "Dis-
cover the Worlds of Alaska," Alaska travel index,
color booklet on Alaska, rockhound information, including clubs and rock dealers.

ARIZONA

Travel Promotion Department, State of Arizona Development Board, 3443 North Central Ave., Phoenix, AZ
85012. "Arizona Rockhound Guide" is a color folder
with pictures of minerals, maps and charts of where to
find them (also gold).

ARKANSAS

Arkansas Department of Parks and Tourism, Dept. 1211,
One Capitol Mall, Little Rock, AR 72201. Special
Rockhound's Vacation Planning Kit, with tour book,
map, state park brochure. You can call, toll-free,
(800) 643-8383, to get one.

COLORADO

State of Colorado, Div. of Commerce & Development, Office of Tourism, 1313 Sherman, Room 500, Denver, CO
80203. Folder of events, large map, dude ranches,
Colorado Adventure Guide, Colo. Outdoor Guide (incl.
gold panning & rockhounding).

GEORGIA

Georgia Bureau of Industry & Trade, P.O. Box 38097,
Atlanta, GA 30334. Gold panning information.

IDAHO

Division of Tourism & Industrial Development, Room
108, Capitol Building, Boise, ID 83720. "Idaho Gemstone Guide." Also, Idaho event schedule, travel accommodations & restaurant guide, state map, color
booklet of attractions, parks & outdoor recreation
guide (incl. rockhound areas).

MICHIGAN

Travel Bureau, Michigan Dept. of Commerce, P.O. Box
30226, Law Building, Lansing, MI 48909. Travel event
guide, traffic law guide, map, museum brochure, color
booklet with addresses for more information.

MINNESOTA

Minnesota Tourism Division Information Center, 48
Cedar St., St. Paul, MN 55101. Brochure, "Rocks &
Minerals of Minnesota," with color photos and map.

MISSOURI

Missouri Division of Tourism, 308 East High St., P.O.
Box 1055, Jefferson City, MO 65102. "Mo. Travel Guide"
gives addresses for information on eight areas in
state; booklet of discount coupons for hotels, food,
camping, etc.

MONTANA

Montana Travel Promotion Unit, Helena, MT 59601.
Large map, rockhound information, mine leaflets.

NEBRASKA

Nebraska Dept. of Economic Development, Division of
Travel and Tourism, 301 Centennial Mall South, Box
94666, Lincoln, NE 68509. "Nebraskaland Magazine,"
with card to send for more info., tourist attractions,
camping areas, state map.

NEVADA

Department of Economic Development, Carson City, NV
89710. Leaflet, "Nevada Rock Hunting," map, color
brochure on Nevada, camping guide, rock club addresses.

NEW HAMPSHIRE

The Lakes Region Assoc., P.O. Box 300-AF, Wolfeboro, NH 03894. Color book, "Where to...in the Lakes Region of N.H.," book on Centre Harbor, Moultonboro, "Weirs Beach," and 8 other brochures. Send 25¢ for postage.

N. H. Vacations, P.O. Box 856, Concord, NH 03301. N.H. events & attractions, lodging & dining, map of state, book, "N. H., We're Better Natured," with other ad- dresses to write to; coupons for more information.

NEW YORK

Travel Bureau, 99 Washington Ave., Albany, NY 12245. Brochure, "Gems of New York State," with map showing gem locations.

"I Love N.Y." Summer Vacations, P.O. Box 808-243, Latham, NY 12110.

NORTH CAROLINA

Mitchell County Chamber of Commerce, 208 Oak Ave., Spruce Pine, NC 28777. Color folder of attractions; guide to shops, restaurants, events; list of mines and map; Crabtree Emerald Mine.

North Carolina Travel Development Section, P.O. Box 27678, Raleigh, NC 27611. Information Bulletin #137, "North Carolina Gems," map and accommodations direc- tory, tour guide, calendar of events, booklet on N.C.

NORTH DAKOTA

North Dakota Tourism Promotion, 1050 E. Interstate Ave., Bismark, ND 58505. Color booklet on N.D.; City- to-City Guide, incl. motels, campgrounds, places to visit; map; fat book of coupons (many free things).

OREGON

The Travel Information Section, Oregon State Highway Division, 101 State Highway Bldg., Salem, OR 97310. "Oregon Rocks, Fossils, Minerals," includes club addresses; color booklet on Oregon attractions.

RHODE ISLAND

Rhode Island Dept. of Economic Development, 7 Jackson Walkway, Providence, RI 02903. Guide to R.I., incl. events, places, accommodations, rock club meetings and shows; folder on Newport mansions; large map of state.

SOUTH CAROLINA

S. C. Division of Tourism, P.O. Box 71, Columbia, SC
29202-0071. Visitor's Guide to S.C., with calendar of
events; postcard for more information; large color
book of things to see, campgrounds, golf courses, and
addresses of local Chambers of Commerce for more info.

SOUTH DAKOTA

South Dakota Division of Tourism, 221 South Central,
Pierre, SD 57501. "S.D. Vacation Guide" includes
rockhound guide, accommodations, camping, things to
see; road map; color brochures on state attractions.

TEXAS

State Department of Highways, Travel & Information
Division, P.O. Box 5064, Austin, TX 78763. Big, color
book, "Texas," includes a rockhound guide.

Chamber of Commerce, 700 Bessemer, Llano, TX 78643.
Information for rockhounds--where to go and whom to
contact for permission to dig.

UTAH

Beaver County Travel Council, P.O. Box 392, Beaver, UT
84713. Information on roads, digging sites, accommodations.

The Garfield Information Center, Panguitch, UT 84759.
Color folder on Bryce Canyon & other attractions, list
of motels, restaurants, etc.; detailed directions to
four places to hunt rocks for free.

VERMONT

Vermont Agency of Development & Community Affairs,
Montpelier, VT 05602. Pamphlet, "Rockhounding in
Vermont."

VIRGINIA

Virginia State Travel Service, 6 North Sixth St.,
Richmond, VA 23219. Large color book of attractions,
postcard for more information.

WASHINGTON

Westport-Grayland Chamber of Commerce, Box 306, Westport, WA 98595. Phone (206) 268-9422. Be specific about the activities you are interested in, so they can send the right material.

WYOMING

Wyoming Travel Commission, Frank Norris Jr. Travel Center, Cheyenne, WY 82002. Book on Wyoming accommodations, map, color book on Wyoming.

CANADA: Provincial and Territorial Offices

Travel Alberta, Box 2500, Edmonton, Alberta T5J 2Z4

Tourism British Columbia, 1117 Wharf St., Victoria, B.C. V8W 2Z2

Travel Manitoba, Dept. 1021, Legislative Bldg., Winnipeg, Manitoba R3C 0V8 Call collect (204) 944-3777.

Tourism New Brunswick, P.O. Box 12345, Fredericton, N.B. E3B 5C3

Dept. of Tourism, P.O. Box 2016, St. John's, Newfoundland A1C 5R8

Travel Arctic, Yellowknife, Northwest Territories X1A 2L9

Nova Scotia: Tourists Information, 129 Commercial St., Portland, Maine 04101 (U.S.A.) Phone (800) 565-6096, Maine Residents (800) 492-0643 [toll-free numbers].

Ontario Travel, 900 Bay St., Queen's Park, Toronto, Ont. M7A 2E5. Phone (800) 828-8585, New York Residents (800) 462-8404 [toll-free numbers].

Visitor Services, P.O. Box 940, Charlottetown, Prince Edward Island C1A 7M5

Tourisme Québec, C.P. 20000, Québec G1K 7X2

Saskatchewan Travel, 3211 Albert St., Regina, Sask. S4S 5W6

Tourism Yukon, P.O. Box 2703, Whitehorse, Yukon Y1A 2C6

Note: The correct form of address for Canada has the postal code after the name of the country. For example: Travel Alberta, Box 2500, Edmonton, Alberta, Canada T5J 2Z4

BOOKS, MAPS, & OTHER PUBLICATIONS

Listed in this section are additional information sources that may be of use to collectors. Since most of them refer to only one state, they are grouped according to the areas involved. Some publications that do not relate to a specific area are grouped together at the beginning of the listing. Ordering information for each publication is provided at the end of its listing.

Fossil Report, P.O. Box 1600, Alamogordo, NM 88310. This is a monthly newsletter about fossils and fossil collecting. Free except for postage. Send stamp for sample.

Gold Deposit Maps: Four maps altogether; one for North Carolina, one for Virginia, one for Georgia, and one for Alabama and South Carolina together, by Mr. Charles Overby. Maps are 37"x24" in size, show several hundred sites, describe how to pan for gold, tell where to look, what equipment is needed, and give a short history of gold in the area. $6.00 per map from Big Ten, Inc., P.O. Box 1231, Cocoa Beach, FL 32931.

Laws & Regulations: Gem, Mineral & Gold Collector's Guide to Mineral Laws & Regulations, by Lanny R. Ream. © 1981. 5 1/4" x 8 1/2" paperback, 67 pages. Regulations and laws concerning collecting & mining, patenting a claim, and collecting antiquities. Bibliography included. Order from the author at P.O. Box 1154, Coeur d'Alene, Idaho 83814. $4.95 plus 63¢ postage.

CALIFORNIA

California Field Trips, by John V. Burris. © 1978. 8 1/2" x 11", 35 pages. Very detailed information on 22 field trips--maps, directions, tools needed, camping information. Order from Mr. Vernon Korstad, 17917 Beardsley St., Castro Valley, CA 94546. $2.75, postpaid.

DELAWARE

Delaware Fossils, by Edward M. Lauginiger and Eugene F. Hartstein. © 1981. 5 7/8" x 9", 38 pages. Description of Cretaceous period in Delaware, fossil locations, descriptions, and drawings of Delaware fossils. Bibliography included. Order from Mr. Edward Lauginiger, 11W Holly Oak Road, Wilmington, DE 19809. $3.25, postpaid.

FLORIDA

Florida Rock and Mineral Trails, by George Heusser. © 1980.
5 1/2" x 8 1/2", 25 pages. Short description of Florida
geology, list of rocks and minerals and locations, list
of mining companies that may permit collecting. Illustrations of Florida fossils, and three maps. Order
from the author at Rt 6, 8079 Breeze Dr., N. Ft. Myers,
FL 33903. $2.50, postpaid.

IDAHO

Idaho Minerals, by Lanny R. Ream. © 1982. 8 1/2" x 11",
106 pages (computer printout [1st edition]). Final
bound (2nd) edition to be ready in 1984. Lists minerals
found in Idaho, and their characteristics and localities,
in alphabetical order. Includes a bibliography. Order
from the author at P.O. Box 1154, Coeur d'Alene, Idaho
83814. $14.95 plus $1.00 shipping.

NEBRASKA

University of Nebraska--Lincoln, Conservation and Survey
Division, Institute of Agriculture and Natural Resources,
113 Nebraska Hall, 901 North 17th St., Lincoln, NE 68588-
0517. An extensive assortment of excellent, low-cost
literature is available to help amateur collectors. A
free booklet listing all such publications is available.
The following list is representative of some types, but
only scratches the surface (pardon the pun):

Creepy Critters from Nebraska's Past. Free folder about
trilobites.
Nebraska's Gold Fields. Free folder.
Minerals and Gemstones of Nebraska. 8 1/2" x 11", 80 pages.
Full color pictures of local minerals, maps, collecting
information, mineralogy. Extensively illustrated. $1.00
Record in Rock, A Handbook of the Invertebrate Fossils of
Nebraska. 8 1/2" x 11", 99 pages. Fully illustrated,
all fossils are pictured. $1.00.
Geologic History of Scotts Bluff National Monument. 8 1/2"x
11", 26 pages. How to reach the monument and what to see
there. Extensively illustrated. $1.00.
Geology of Lake McConaughy Area, Keith County, Nebraska.
8 1/2" x 11", 22 pages. Illustrated with maps and photo-
graphs. $1.00.
Geology Along the Republican River Valley Near Red Cloud,
Nebraska. 8 1/2" x 11", 25 pages. Maps, drawings,
illustrations of fossils in the area. $1.00.
A series of "Field Guides," at 25¢ each, is available for
specific areas. They include maps of the area and il-

lustrations of the terrain and of fossils found there.
They are available for the following areas:

Cass County--Weeping Water
Sarpy County--Gretna State Fish Hatchery Area
Gage County--Odell-Krider Area
Thayer County--Alexandria and Gilead Areas
Pawnee County--Table Rock Area
Greeley County--Chalk Mine State Wayside Area
Jefferson County--Fairbury Area

NEW ENGLAND

Gold--How to Find and Pan Gold in New England, by Ernest
Foley. © 1980. 5 1/4" x 8 1/4", 16 pages. Detailed
instructions for a beginner on how to find and recover
gold in New Hampshire and Vermont. Maps of places to
pan and descriptions of many gold sites. Order from
the author at R.F.D. #2, Woodsville, NH 03785. Cost is
$3.00 plus 35¢ for mailing.

NEW MEXICO

New Mexico Geology, c/o New Mexico Bureau of Mines,
Socorro, NM 87801. A magazine for professional geolo-
gists and science teachers. Write for sample copy.

New Mexico Rocks & Minerals, the Collecting Guide, by Frank
S. Kimbler and Robert J. Narsavage, Jr. © 1981. 5 1/2"x
8 1/2", 71 pages. Contains 23 pages of maps of collecting sites, plus a list of New Mexico Mining Districts
with minerals found. Color pictures of local minerals,
list of mine locations and addresses, map and mineral
index. Order from New Mexico Co., P.O. Box 41997, Chi-
cago, IL 60641. $7.50.

NEW JERSEY

Minerals of Laurel Hill, Secaucus, New Jersey, by Nicholas
W. Facciolla. 1981. 6" x 9", 48 pages. Gives the history, geology, and mineralogy of Laurel Hill (formerly
Snake Hill). Many photos of minerals and the area. (No
collecting is now allowed.) Available from the author
at 50 Maple St., Teaneck, NJ 07666. $3.50 plus $1.00
postage and handling.

NEW YORK

Gold, Silver, and Other Mines of the Shawangunks, by George
Heusser. © 1976. 5 1/2" x 8 1/2", 38 pages. A history

of gold, lead, zinc, and copper mines near Kingston and
Ellenville, N.Y. Map shows mine locations. Includes
a bibliography and index. Order from the author at
Rt. 6, 8079 Breeze Dr., N. Ft. Myers, FL 33903. $2.50,
postpaid.

NORTH CAROLINA

Gold Mining and Rubies Too, by Merrill Hewitt. © 1980.
5 1/4" x 8", 31 pages. Information, directions, and
maps to nine mines in North Carolina. Illustrations
and other information about gold mining and ruby mining
in the area. Available from the author at Rt. 2, Box
272, Franklin, NC 28734. $2.95

The Cowee Valley Ruby Mining Story, by René Fafard. © 1965,
1979. 6" x 9", 23 pages. Information for visitors to
Cowee Valley ruby mines. Map, how to mine, properties
of ruby crystals, and illustration of crystal shapes.
Many illutrations. Order from K. Fafard, Rt. 4, Box
481, Franklin, NC 28734. $2.00, postpaid.

OREGON

The Rockhound's Map of Oregon. © 1982. 17 1/2" x 22 1/2".
A map of the state with 70 mineral locations given, and
directions for finding each one (in addition to being
shown on the map). Also includes advice about each
site. Available from Highland Rock & Gift Shop, 1316
Hines Blvd., Burns, OR 97720. $2.00, postpaid.

WASHINGTON

Handbook for Gold Prospectors in Washington, by Wayne C.
Moen and Marshall T. Huntting. 1975. Complete gold
mining information; staking a claim, testing for gold,
panning, building a sluice box, and many gold locations
in the state. Originally published by the State of
Washington Dept. of Natural Resources (Information Circular 57). Now available from Pearl Electronics, Inc.,
312 Dexter Ave. N., Seattle, WA 98109. 8 1/2" x 11",
90 pages, including Bibliography and Property Index.
$10.00, postpaid ($7.95 plus $2.05 shipping & handling).

Minerals of Washington, by Bart Cannon. © 1975. 5 1/2" x
8 1/2", 184 pages. Describes 400 mineral species and
notes their occurrence at nearly 1000 locations across
the state. Also contains about 100 illustrations, including several maps. Large bibliography. Available
from the author at 1041 N.E. 100 St., Seattle, WA 98125.
$6.95, postpaid.

The Rockhound's Map of Washington. © 1971. 17 1/2" x
20 1/2". A collection of 21 small maps on one large
sheet, with directions to more than 32 locations; includes advice, hours open, fees, camping information,
and exact driving instructions. Available from Highland Rock & Gift Shop, 1316 Hines Blvd., Burns, OR
97720. $1.00, postpaid.

WYOMING

Wyoming Geological Survey, Box 3008, University Station,
University of Wyoming, Laramie, WY 82071. Publishes a
series of handbooks of interest to rock collectors.
They are $3.00 each. Titles include:
Traveler's Guide to the Geology of Wyoming
Minerals and Rocks of Wyoming
Fossils of Wyoming
Caves of Wyoming
Thermal Springs of Wyoming

CANADA

Geological Survey of Canada, 601 Booth Street, Ottawa, Ontario, Canada K1A 0E8. Information for Collectors, re-
vised annually, provides (in English and French) a list
of currently available publications of the Geological
Survey of Canada. The Rocks and Minerals for the Collector series of handbooks alone covers many areas in
13 volumes still in print. Many other guidebooks and
valuable sources of information for collectors are
listed. Information for Collectors is available free
of charge, from the address listed above.

Ontario Government Book Store, 880 Bay St., Toronto, Ontario, Canada M5S 1Z8 can supply the following books:

Geological Guide Book No. 2, Geology and Scenery, North
Shore of Lake Superior, by E. G. Pye, Ontario Division
of Mines. 140 pages.
Geological Guide Book No. 4, Geology and Scenery, North
Shore of Lake Huron Region, by J. A. Robertson and K.
D. Card, Ontario Division of Mines. 224 pages.

Peterson Guide to Mineral Collecting--Bancroft Area, by
Helen Peterson. Second Edition, © 1978. 5 1/2" x
8 1/2", 61 pages. Much good advice about rock collecting in the Bancroft area; directions to 101 sites,
keyed to a highway map and your speedometer. List of
minerals, indexed to locations. Centerfold is an area
map. Available from the author at Box 1386, Bancroft,
Ontario, Canada K0L 1C0. $4.50, postpaid.

ISBN 0-943502-03-9